Inheritance of Flowers

Inheritance of Flowers

Poems by

Charise M. Hoge

© 2025 Charise M. Hoge. All rights reserved.
This material may not be reproduced in any form, published,
reprinted, recorded, performed, broadcast,
rewritten, or redistributed without
the explicit permission of Charise M. Hoge.
All such actions are strictly prohibited by law.

Cover design by Shay Culligan
Cover image by Sylvia Rago
Author photo by Charise M. Hoge

ISBN: 978-1-63980-729-1

Kelsay Books
502 South 1040 East, A-119
American Fork, Utah 84003
Kelsaybooks.com

for
my grandmother's
flower lore

Acknowledgments

Many thanks go to my dear fellow poets of the Capitol Hill Poetry Group. They listen with care, advise well, and help improve my work.

My gratitude goes to family and friends who nurture this writing life. Joshua Miller, you have my heartfelt thanks for supporting the arts in Hardy County, West Virginia and commissioning the poem "Art in an Age of Uncertainty."

If a place can be thanked, my abode in the mountains of Lost River, WV is most deserving. The forest is a haven for wandering, the pond is fresh for swimming, and the view never gets old. Inspiration is easy to catch here.

Grateful acknowledgment is made to the editors of the following publications where these poems first appeared:

The American Scholar "Next Line, Please" poetry column:
   "Rampant Writing," "Couples Fugue," "Le Petit Prince"
Beyond Words Literary Magazine: "Good Riddance," "Full Stop"
Cathexis Northwest Press: "Flashback"
Englyn Journal: "Wayword"
High Shelf Press: "Onrush," "Art in an Age of Uncertainty"
Innisfree Poetry Journal: "Roaming"
Next Line, Please: Prompts to Inspire Poets and Writers: "Return"
The Pine Cone Review: "The Dance Performance"
These Fragile Lilacs: "Ours"
Tiny Seed Literary Journal: "To Do or Not to Do"
Topical Poetry: "Anointed"
Tuck Magazine: "Lost"

Contents

i. roots & rootlessness

Rampant Writing	17
Future Plans	18
Tropical	20
Pivotal Grace	21
Scene at the Tate	22
Almost	23
A Child's Piety	24
Boxed Corsages	25
Flower Child	26
The Reading	27
Audition	28
Scissors	29
Study Break	30
Lost	31
Braiding	32
This Side of Iraq	34
Onrush	35
121 Heatherdown Road	36
Taboo	37
Ours	38
Couples Fugue	39
Roaming	40
Higher Ground	42
Good Riddance	43
Wallpaper	44
Full Stop	45
Well-Read Rubáiyát	46
Once an Intern	47
Wayword	48

ii. hibernation

Woo the Day	51
Spring Sequestered	52
Night Shift	53
Bird's-Eye View	54
Art in an Age of Uncertainty	55
Earth Tone	56
December	57
At Home	58
Wholly, Holy	59
Friction	60
Absurd Lovebird	61
My Love Affair with Trees	62
Tethered	63
Cumbersome Summer	64

iii. gardens after gardens

Return	67
Upending	68
Rosary	70
Flashback	71
Anointed	73
Canto do Poeta	74
The Dance Performance	75
Reptilian Morning	76
Excursion	78
Le Petit Prince	79
Haecceity	80
Spiel	81

To Do or Not to Do	82
An Understanding	83
Bryant Park, Midtown	84
Answer	85
My Visitation	86
Afterward	87
Notes	89

Don't go outside your house to see flowers.
My friend, don't bother with that excursion.
Inside your body there are flowers.
One flower has a thousand petals.

—Kabir

i. roots & rootlessness

Rampant Writing

no one will read . . . for poets
are cropping up like a luxury

of weeds: sagebrush, mugwort, nettle;
not the sort of plant anyone chooses
for plots aiming to be garden beds,

but the kind that catches by
surprise,

causes sneezing
that creates a seismic shift
along cranial synarthroses,

refocusing the eyes, and somewhere
someone will say "bless you"

Future Plans

My pseudonym
had a ring to it.
Stage name
for a star.
Gloria.
Followed by Flowers.
Gloria Flowers.

We were staging skits
at my patio and yours.
A fairy tale. A western.
Inviting neighbors
for "summer theatre."

Until the schism—
a best friend split.
Then puberty set in,
snug and foreign.
Like the backdrop
of Vietnam.
Which was constant.
A faint heartbeat.

It stops beating
during assembly,
as the headmaster
announces
that the war has ceased.
News sounding
like an apology.
A hush of disbelief.

We file out holding
hymnals,
filling hallways
with our untrained
voices: *Gloria, Gloria!*
Soldiers gone,
gone to flowers, every one.

Tropical

I remember being superimposed
upon the world—
as if it hadn't caught up to me
or I hadn't caught up to it—
standing next to a broad-leaf plant
that dwarfed me
in a dress that flared out from my legs
making something of a mushroom
out of my three-year-old self.

I remember my father behind the camera
but I didn't smile or pose
because I was superimposed—
with petticoat gills
and a whitish-blonde cap of hair,
white t-strap sandals coalescing toes,
standing in the sun's glare.

I remember feeling *more than*—
outside of my diminutive size,
flowing in the mycelium underfoot
or the airy galaxy—
as the camera clicked in a cul-de-sac
on a hill above the busy avenue
where the rainforest
lies within city limits and the canal
is one of the seven wonders—
dressed for a portrait,
ancient in my raw materials.

Pivotal Grace

Backstage
where flowers bloom
in dressing rooms,

where costume and rouge
are prepped hours before
the house opens doors,

there is nothing to do
but think: you aren't sure
you remember
the sequence of moves.

As expectant as faces
in a theatre darkening,
you're vacant, a vase . . .

where flowers bloom
in dressing rooms,
backstage.

Scene at the Tate

There are rumors in the gallery.
Strangers talk about what was staged—
the model with silver gown stayed hours in a tin tub,
laid out like caviar—to the general view, a maiden voyage.
And Millais, Pre-Raphaelite, realist to the manner born,
grappled with the Surrey flies, windy gusts, and notice
for trespassing—murder most foul of the hay.
He confided to a friend, "painting of a picture under such
circumstances would be greater punishment to a murderer
than hanging." Not to mention the medical bill for Siddal
of the bath, as warmth elapsed for the sake of painstaking
detail. Art exacts a price and so the heart—
Ophelia floats in her perpetual spring.

Almost

       is a sacred qualifier.
Between it and the fatal
"_____ lost her"
are intervening deities, riddles.

       is an almighty rebound:
morning's lark,
cereal for breakfast,
fret over finals,

      the f word,
      the F train,
      fog of warm breath,

            angel's breadth
            melting into the back
            of a fresh start.

A Child's Piety

Snowbound. Here in the Upper Hudson Valley.
    The accumulation steady while the wind
        stacks heaps throughout the neighborhood.

Awake to the landscape of a new planet.
    The front door opens to a storm door that won't budge;
        snow pressed against glass like a cresting wave.

How a circular driveway melds with two halves
    of the yard, black tips of lampposts
        marking former bounds.

A side door, to the patio, lets a neighbor deliver
    goods—and lets a gaggle outside.
        Stay until fingers and toes beg for warmth.

Icy mittens rest on a radiator to dry. Nightfall
    comes fast. Moonlight on snow crystals is church.
        Gaze at winter's altar from a window. Spellbound.

Boxed Corsages

It was old-fashioned, or typically
Southern, or simply what was done

—corsages for Easter Sunday service.
Pinned on new dresses, shaded by new hats.

No other family had this predicament
at St. Peter's of Albany, N.Y.

A Tennessee idea boxed in our fridge.
From grandma Ida Mae, the florist.

Delivered to our mom, my sister, and me.
Ladies three, though I was pre-teen.

Showy, pesky as a spider could be
—we complained.

Overcome, our mom shut the Frigidaire.
Her day of reckoning,

as grandma's corsages lay cold.
There was praise for the risen

and white lilies for the altar—
the year we welcomed white lies.

Flower Child

New York. And the sixties are over.
The promise of a career as a flower child
fades, like anything that's fresh picked.

Cut gladioli are the mainstay of every funeral
spray. Even for Elvis, a customer at Mama
Burke's floral shop on S. Bellevue, Memphis.

It's all arranged. Mom and I will move back
to the "Home of the Blues" before my freshman
year. Then the family can track her eccentricities.

For one summer I make bows, water whatever
grows in the greenhouse, dress potted plants
in cellophane, strip thorns from long-stemmed roses.

Love-struck. We meet on the bridge to campus.
You are a musician. I want to be girl.
Not the pains of a woman.

The Reading

She had the credentials
to recite at the library
poetry reading.

A demeanor well composed,
while each poem closed
with a smile tight to her mouth.

I thought of a cat that's trapped
a mouse. Another poem . . .
another mouse.

Without a doubt the writing
was adept. But her satisfaction
. . . mmm . . . a tour de force.

Audition

with apologies to Gerard Manley Hopkins

On stage, at the boys' military academy,
I recite while seated in my uniform:
white collared shirt tucked into leaf green skirt,
matching green socks stretched thin from tugging,
and brown buckle shoes. I press my knees together
for integrity.

The poem of my choice is "Carrion Comfort"
which I have never uttered aloud. Gambling on
the intonation of "thy wring-world right foot rock?"
my voice is a filly cantering on a carousel,
stuck in the whirl of an incessant band organ.

Rows of boys I have looked at fleetingly, and
a cadre of girls who have something to assert—
like buoyant breasts or popularity—watch me read.
"Scan with darksome devouring eyes my bruisèd bones?"
I'm losing my chance at the high school play.

Feeling uneasy, queasy—"me heaped there;
me frantic to avoid thee and flee?"
—as the final phrase disbands in dismay,
"I wretch lay wrestling with (my God!) my God."

Scissors

Shopkeepers wore them on chains like necklaces

at the fabric store where I tagged along with my mother.
She was sewing clothes for us

at four and seven years old. Maybe not all of our clothes,
but smart outfits and Halloween get-ups.

One year she dressed me as cupid's heart with an arrow piercing

through cardboard—an announcement, of sorts, that my own small
heart had a hole in it. From birth.

It's not clear whether I wandered out of her sight or she wandered
out of mine when a scissors lady accosted me,

leaned low with the cutting tool swaying oh-so menacingly.

My screams brought my mother back. The instant she was there
everything was fine. But no one understood

the horror. As if it never happened. It happened more than once.
The first time she was hospitalized,

nurses confiscated a small pair of scissors she kept in her purse.

Rules and protocol. I stood by, in my school blazer
beneath fluorescent lights.

Staff were no-nonsense as I held my ragged self together.
Like a grown-up.

Study Break

spring   like another
when the future   spreads out
flush   as a field
first times   for such   and such
seemingly   far   looming soon

outside the classroom   books set
aside   the dandelions   call
my name

plentiful yellow   deigning
to pop up   as I bellyflop   to them
knot their stems

round round   for a tiara
to wear   the rest of   an afternoon

Lost

for Christine Blasey Ford

It's not exact . . .
where her novel life was headed
or could have been or would be
going toward a middle
of its beginning.
That course extinguishes
when she's taken
as a temporary novelty.
No wonder she can't remember
how she got home
after.

Braiding

Alongside the plaits
wound and clipped
together at the nape
of the neck
there's another/same
person remembering
this wreath of hair
as her own,
sees her well-traveled
cheek rest against
this earnest face
at the crux of nineteen

Alongside the lap
of the sea
an iguana waddles
in then out of view
ocean wide as decades
where a book floats
to the mind's surface . . .
Spencer's *Faerie Queene*
quests and questions
discussed at a round table
in Renaissance Lit.
at the crux of nineteen

Alongside the mantle
of middle age
is an island tale . . .
chivalry of mangroves:
their yellowing leaves
act as saltwater filters
to defend their green,
marrying loss with growth
and growth with loss
braid after braid after braid
some chapters yet to read
at the crux of nineteen

This Side of Iraq

Waiting,
partaking of the day,
knowing
there's always this back door
to another view
that never closes,
that sends a chill
anytime.

So even when I sit
at my desk,
at our table,
or with anyone,
I don't know which way I'm facing.

In my exposure
I'm captive to the countdown
from the last time I saw you
to the next time.
And the longer you survive,
the better you are at surviving,
I begin to wonder what will end
when next time is now.

Onrush

In the recovery of words
some are birds,

a covey of adjectives:
full-throated, backlit, furtive,

without the testimony of verbs.

121 Heatherdown Road

In the so-long's
sometime now gone
of a Georgia summer,
sealed boxes on a liner
to Southeast Asia,
I stand in the hallway
of a dwelling that is ours
and not ours, as a tour
of duty calls. I am stalling.
Seconds I am stealing
as my right hand at 33
brushes the wall, sorry
to dash so soon. Our hearth
remains . . . a downy start.
I swipe what clings: the if-
onlys, the new lease on life.
It's now rent-to-own, foster
sort of deal, a borrowed nest.
The tenants barge in. I watch,
wallflower to their scattershot
steps and echoes. No sofas,
settees, cushions, to be at ease.

Taboo

Outside the pantomime of living rooms,
outside a perimeter of nonchalance,
another territory looms . . .
with its lush foliage and native dance.

Outside a perimeter of nonchalance,
I lean into pauses of your sentences
with their lush foliage and native dance.
You are listening for how I listen.

I lean. In the pauses of your sentences,
another territory looms.
I am listening for how you listen,
outside the pantomime of living rooms.

Ours

This refuge
we foraged

from vines
stemming
to conspire union

in a near grasp,

from twine
of leaving
tightening slack

in a haunted clasp,

on milkweed insistence
to cross distances

stands like a ruin
bewildering the plain

Couples Fugue

Every marriage tends to consist of an aristocrat and a peasant.
—John Updike

In every marriage one is royal while the other is loyal.
One and other rotate periodically around a periodic table
. . . the royal sits at the head, loyal at the side, until a fugue
starts a round of musical chairs; and this is where they
see eye to eye, watching each other for a cue to stop
the music, as if the royal or the loyal were an impostor,
and a wizened magician composed of the chemistry
that attracted them at first wields a staff that wriggles
like a snake . . . smack in the middle of their shenanigans.

Roaming

I'm a room

that houses a quiet choir.
The anticipated organist
latent to arrive. He—
it must be "he"—
has forgotten us.
I assume.

A room of assuming.
Rustling garb, glances
to & fro. Time passes like
color fading.

A room of color fading.
I failed art from the get-go,
adding paint on paint
until my paper looked brown.
Layers dulling.

A room of dulling.
In first grade I hummed,
without knowing that I hummed.
The teacher had me stand,
walk and hum between desks.
Pilloried, at six.

A room at six.
My mom toweling me dry
after a bath. I shake
my nakedness. To move like this
is not nice. My naughty body stops.

A room that stops.
The choir gone to seed.
Nothing other than a sweep
of heather, bracken, peat.

I'm a moor.

Higher Ground

for Khet Thi and the others

Follow a vine . . .
climbing through empty nymph casings of Brood X
summer droplets of rain in the Northern Hemisphere
plastic sheaths of tossed newspapers

The World section coverage of a strange exodus
"Northbound Wild Elephant Eating and Walking Tour"
bordering Myanmar a herd has left its habitat

military coup quashes new flowering of freedoms
underfoot a *cri de coeur* ignored is quivering
toward higher ground the call is borne

ghosted poets are carried on the backs of pachyderms
away from a host of atrocities away from
disquieting lands to become legend

Good Riddance

When you release a crystal ball into the wild,
there are no rules.

It doesn't have to be during a full moon;
it could be broad daylight

in the middle of the week.
There may not be any howling dogs

or cloud of bats, or an ounce
of concoction or mystifying

incantations or fog.
Choose your spot—it doesn't require much

acreage. A public garden will do.
Here—at the base of a tree behind a bench

where it settles innocent as a pearl
off the strand of a choker

that never quite fit.
A forecast that dogged you

put to rest. Wish it well.
No fanfare is necessary when

you walk away—
even if you're getting increasingly luminous.

Wallpaper

It was a thoroughfare,
my bedroom. Access on both sides:
toward parents, toward sister.
Within, wooden butterfly
wings support a glass top table.
Against the wall, a mock phone booth.
Mod. Late 60s early 70s style.
Green and yellow color scheme.

Gone was the original pink carpet
and pale walls. My wallpaper
popped in stripes and bright flowers.
As snazzy as the orange minidress
and green fishnet stockings worn
for the first day of fifth grade.

A mismatched area of my ceiling
confessed the effort to make
the pattern meet. My mother
papered it herself, a project
begun by showing me samples.
We were in cahoots for decorating.
Left with not-quite-right results.

The loud look became dated
when it was just the two of us.
Sister off to college, father
to a condo. Our household a whisper
of itself. The weighted wings,
mocking phone. And the tryst with
an inconspicuous journal at my bed.

Full Stop

joy, anyway

miniscule as a field pea

pebble out of a tidal wave

joy, anyway

sweet-talking to stay

round to a full stop, period.

Joy. Any way.

Miniscule as a field pea.

Well-Read Rubáiyát

Saturday, returning footwear that failed
to fit my father's swollen feet.
In the store mirror, some version of myself,
stretched long—a tall woman, flustered.

The moving finger writes, and having writ, moves on

Confronting the finality of being fully grown.
Now. Now that my hands scrunch his sock
so it can move over toes first, then sole
and heel, then zigzag up to the ankle.

nor all your Piety nor Wit shall lure it back to cancel half a Line

Omar Khayyam's words are his, by heart.
Today, something new. At 92. "I'm getting old."
He has his wits about him to witness the frailty.
Watching, unflinching.

nor all your Tears wash out a Word of it.

The child I was knocks about my psyche,
unsettled. When his back complained, my father
stopped carrying me up to bed. "Last time"
—words he exhaled while setting me down.

Once an Intern

She's art now.

Sculpted of subway tiles
circa Manhattan 1980s
meshed with textiles:

t-shirt with cutout scoop
neckline slouching a smile
shoulder to shoulder

& white skirt splurge buy
from Betsy Johnson,
snap studded placket plus
lace hem; shoeless, poised

for modern dance studios—
92nd street Y, Hawkins down
5th Ave. Greenwich Village

   no hairstyle, coifed
with a beige bell lampshade
earned as a clerk at the job
fit between hours of training,

circles of inpatients in the Bronx.

Wayword

Romance is at the edge
of everything, where shrouds
shrug their seams to unravel.
It's never clean.

ii. hibernation

Woo the Day

At first light,
day is a foal

no one owns.
Newborn,

ready to stand.
Riderless.

Carpe diem,
your "giddy-up,"

breaks it in.
Saddled, day

likens to a lady
sashaying down

boulevards,
avenues, byways.

The sass of day
is everlasting.

Head held high,
horseshoes littered

like luck, leaving
you her trappings.

Spring Sequestered

after William Blake

for the hours perusing
my backyard

while we cannot traverse
the world,

lilies of the valley profess
a governance of air

from a square below a bay
window

along a slope beside lopsided
slate stones

meant for stepping
—hours that have stooped

interminable, I see eternity
in a flower

Night Shift

When comfort divorces you,

whether or not
this was warranted,
whether or not you assumed
there was some guarantee,
whether or not you saw
this coming,

you want to go back
to normal that's torn asunder.

When you lose your footing,

whether or not you brace—
unsteady as a toddler,
whether or not you name
this a 'new normal'
to escape the guesswork,

this is freefall;

you launch into the dark
like a moth, not
particularly lovely,
taking on the night shift
of pollination
as each nocturnal
jasmine opens, opens—

whether or not you can sleep,
beauty will be
consuming the darkness.

Bird's-Eye View

An argument of birds
still sounds like song
though our daughter
says we're bickering
March 2020 into April
as we quarantine

from the brush of society.
She's missing the point.
How husbandwifery
hashes out territorial right
through a thicket of sharing.
We're still in the fight,

off-pitch or off-key,
clashing with complacency.

Art in an Age of Uncertainty

for Joshua Miller

Theatre-in-the-round, Shakespeare in the Park,
opening night, live concert will be cancelled.

Premiere, bookstore reading, arts festival, gallery show,
museum exhibit, new release will be cancelled.

The readers, actors, dancers,
visual artists, musicians will stay home.

The paintings will not be viewed. The poetry will not be spoken.
The dance will not be staged. The music will not be heard.

We will wear masks, without costumes.
Grocery stores will have lines, without tickets.
Health care workers will be given applause, without reservation.

We will be held in captivity,
while sheep roam the unpeopled village streets.

We will sit, scrounge, stockpile, stake out a living, sanitize.
We will surrender to the foreign country we've become.
We will be strangers to strangeness.

Spacing will be six feet apart in public, and in private we will pace
. . . to and from doorways, up or down staircases, around furniture.

Forward momentum will loop back, with more curves in each path.
The Golden Ratio will restring the musician's instrument

and arch the dancer's back. The sculptor will render a sunflower
from the whirlpool effect. And the poet will extract black ink
from the center of our spiraling.

Earth Tone

We set out to knead the mountain

  while it gives

before the crusty surface hardens

  while it leavens

orange yellow reddish leaves

  while fall turns

round like the wind-up of a music box

  while it plays

the same song yearly, more dear

  while we recall

forgetting how the season waltzes in

December

Less
and less
delicious warmth

as winter unwraps
its grey forlorn.

Also
—O also,
sotto voce—

a silver gleam adorns
the boughs bereft

to say, like a dare, *adore me*.

At Home

I am astounded by the mundane.

By the dishwasher stacked and ready to run.

By clothes clean, dry, in the dresser or closet.

By the bed made.

By the makings of a meal on hand.

By the arrangement of table linens.

I am astounded by the mundane.

For there is metamorphosis in a menial task.

For there is enough to sustain this small life.

For there is metamorphosis.

For there is enough.

For this small life.

I am astounded by the mundane.

Wholly, Holy

In the betwixt, the cling, the dismay,
our ends are frayed.

There is a knot—
call it beloved, dearest whatever
—that can't be bought.

The yarns we spin come tied together.

Friction

Another birthday insists.
    We must tango, says age.

Leonard Cohen has a tune
    to wrap and distract us.

Darling darting legs
    nearly singe, and our gaze

grinds heat from a smoky
    raspy beat.

Like a vintage LP
    we are well played.

Old inhibition aside,
    with no fiction between us.

Absurd Lovebird

She's done
settling in a chair held
mid-air for her—
upholstered with reverie.

Holding court by facsimile.

She's laden
with the fruit
of consequence—
quitting repeated tries.

Each reprise believing.

She's stunned
like a starling stricken
by a windowpane—
'might be' wasn't any place.

Only a rush of urgency.

My Love Affair with Trees

I will not scrawl upon your bark but will sculpt
my body at your base.

I will not transmogrify as dryad or Daphne but will pursue
a deciduous visit.

I will not discriminate based on type but will take note
of your lofty limbs.

Sentient sycamore, oak, tulip, beech, baobab, olive,
lucuma, dawn redwood.

I will not take your stance half-heartedly but will stray
from ground you caress.

I will not demean your significance but will fall
for the next sturdy sort.

I will not forget your stately presence but will follow
your lore transcendent.

Tethered

> *Hope is the thing with feathers*
> —Emily Dickinson

Hope is the thing with tethers
that crouches in the farthest
corner—around a convoluted hall
of darkened interior walls.

      It lies in wait, as in a cavern,
      encampment of the soul.
      Across a groan of distances—
      beside the ghoulish thought,

            there is a beast beneficent.
            Coiled supple in its lair. On the sly,
            will quicken. A pheromone of approach
            —this leap that takes me by the throat.

Cumbersome Summer

Japanese maple masquerades
as an ostrich, those leafy plumes
bushing out atop the slender leg

. . . we did a new planting, digging in
where the grass gave up and died

now the coral bells, astilbes, hostas
rabbits ravage, yet I'm rooting
for this garden to astonish

to come back with a vengeance
the bite taken out of her

to prosper as I hover over
this scrappy patch,
skimpy plumes pining for water,

upturned worm wriggling dirt's desire,
a tiny Eden in the making

and here are two sling-back chairs,
one for you . . . be my companion,
like the ostrich too heavy-laden to fly.

iii. gardens after gardens

Return

I stop somewhere waiting for you,
a few paces from reason.

Like the morning glory, I remember
glorifying the gilded blue of new
spreading welcome.

Giddiness overshadowed
by beckoning back to day's end,
by collapse into creases
the sepal skirt that hemmed
me to the skies of us.

I remember how to decay, a beginning.
I stop waiting for you somewhere.

Upending

for Ukraine

In the teal room
there is no war

a hibiscus winters
here and a jade

spills its succulence
over a ceramic container

amplified in the mirror
jade upon jade

an orange chaise
offers rest

while obsidian chimes
grace a corner

to erase the corner
in the same manner

a width of windows
and glass sliding door

erase the walls
in a room

that could never
be shelter

exposed like the flip
of a page

from one country
to another

as the handbook
of sanctuary

is burned

Rosary

Pink rose in a planter
thrived three winters.

Fourth spring, sprouts absent,
I give it to the sunny plot.

Slim chance of retrieval,
rose spirit sapped.
Charcoal color thorns intact.

Shard of crystal I bury with
the transplant,
banking on reversal.

Even lost causes
have patron saints. I kneel
in the flowerbed, a supplicant.

Flashback

I swim with dragonflies
skittering the surface
of this spring fed pond

at one with my immersion,
reversing a situational gravity
of immense abiding heat

and the claustrophobia
suburbia imparts,
a body in a body of water

in a bowl of earth
in a country that has forsaken
the *my* of body, for the body politic.

Another hot July without air
conditioning I sit in front of the fan
abandoning shirt for red bandeau

ready-made from a headband
stretched across my nine-year-old
chest, for a modicum of modesty.

Two daughters later, first winter
after a stint in Bangkok, snowbanks
cover streets and yards. Girls stream

into our house, dropping hats, gloves,
jackets, boots, socks, snow pants,
sweaters, then shirts and underwear

as they absorb the stuffy heat
and music left playing in the living
room. They skip, jump, turn,

laugh with a giddy girlishness.
Womanhood will startle them
soon enough;

and I relish this reprieve of sanctions.
To be feral in the sanctity of home.
To be home in the *my* of body.

Anointed

for Tyre Nichols

Because they did not see his crown
Because we see it now
Another nobody heading somewhere
Cornered not too far from home
Though farther from than ever
Because they did not see the sign
Because we see it now
Castlegate Lane shown on camera
The castle gate of crossroads
Another someone passes to kingdom

Canto do Poeta

Only fado will do.
Saudade, a far cry from innuendo.
Songs that plummet like a shipwreck
then search to rescue survivors.
She sings, in black lace with bared shoulders
—a figurehead at the prow of a cramped
grotto—swaying us in her hold. A cargo
of souls transported, our last night in Lisboa.

The Dance Performance

A world where walls collapse
to wings, stage left and stage right.
Lights obscure the watchers who
become, collectively, a seated sun.

We warm to you and make offerings,
raise our hearts from their sheathings.
Exposed in the repose of a curve
or twist that turns to fate. A flub

integrates like coarse salt finely ground
into ocean pulsing from the marley
floor. We are swept by purling currents
repeatedly, hurled into place to balance

on pinnacles of rock. Devoted to landing
without calcifying, our poses refashioned
by another surge through the floorboards.

Ovation is dawn rising upon us.
Your applause echoes within the shells
of our bodies well after curtain calls.

Reptilian Morning

Warming before the solstice,
summer isn't squeamish.
A season sliding out of borders

like the lizard peering
from the back of a picture frame
on my wall in the isthmus

of Panama. Mountainous
West Virginia lies far from
the tropics, yet reptiles are surfacing.

Some invisible conductor
is raising the baton—
starting a symphony of emergence.

A box turtle—the type Alexandra
called *Patterns,* and immortalized
in a crayon drawing

—crosses our gravel road
to a flowerbed, where the first
tiger lily has opened.

Two black snakes—helpmates
that hide under the old house—slither
in the direction *Patterns*

left behind. They're showing off
their wavy concertina motion
—sidling up the longer grass,

where resting robins aren't at all
disconcerted. The snapping turtle—
usually reclusive, skittish—

is afloat in a triangle of water, airing
its carapace. Year after year—carefully,
peaceably—we slip in for our swims.

Excursion

Transported by train from Paris to Giverny anticipation
brought me this far, though my sister made the invitation
for a foray into France—she the keen photographer
settles on a bud or a shade, maybe she'll wallpaper
a room with what Monet seeded; we're circling
around his pond with a gait befitting
a cloister, as if we were spying
a leftover paradise pulsing
with perfume, exulting
in our growing tipsy
by the simply

Le Petit Prince

Art: boa constrictor
devours elephant.
For grown-ups—
hat inferred.
Journey knight-like,
lightyears mystical.
Nonsensical orders,
presumptions
questioned.
Rose speaks to us
vis-à-vis
writer Exupéry's
yellow-haired zephyr.

Haecceity

As I stare into the amaryllis
it asks me why was I ever
shy

while I was shrinking
from the squint
of scrutiny

that seemed to measure
what is up to snuff
or pleasing

I was this
—the thisness
of an amaryllis—
no less than magnificent.

Spiel

She could say the mistake was fake
or pour him a little more *saké,*

plead that she's not as sane
as portrayed, not the same

as any synonym for tame,
contained (who doesn't teem

with vicissitudes?), to seem
the rub rather than mending seam,

rather than soothing sonata, to beam
ambiguously. More words for the ream

all mean one thing: she's unmistakably real.

To Do or Not to Do

for Alex

There's a hole in my to do list
which lets me peer through
to the other side of importance
where a murmuring stream
of consciousness
breaks down
what is timebound
like water eroding rock
continuously . . .
the so-called future
mapped out
like geography
becoming flimsy
while the lay of the land
below my windows
shows a gathering of violets
risen from their rhizomes
covering ground better than gossip.

An Understanding

Because, Clematis.
Otherwise, what's the point?
A six-pointed star tantalizes.
Another one opens, unasked.
Flash of a flourish.
Yet, perennial.
Like some friendships.
Showing up. As periwinkle
or blush as ever.
Conversation adds mulch.
Teasing shakes the old petals
down. Stargazing is a twinkle
in the eyes forgiving
your patchy company.
Fondness thrives from beneath
the surface. Bleeds color.

Bryant Park, Midtown

There's a bathroom attendant
who, by miracle of mopping,
makes of a latrine a shrine.

He ushers us from the line
that winds back toward the lions
of the New York Public Library.

It's an orderly procession.
Everyone has their place
while the pace is promising.

Larkspur at the alcove
and orchestral sounds soothe
after the wait. No trace of odors

or footprints. How deftly
the mopping happens,
without trespass or misstep.

Swift and steadfast. No chair
for sitting or bowl for tips.
A pure devotion to task.

In a park named after a poet,
at the public Beaux-Arts
restroom, there's an everyday saint.

Answer

There were ravens making a clatter
on the tin roof above our bed.
We woke unsure of the sound, seeing
a lone black bird in the black walnut tree
. . . then two, then three, perched above
the well behind this farmhouse
not of our ancestors but of a new history
for ourselves and daughters,
something akin to a hundred-acre wood
two and a half hours from Washington, DC.

They took their leave, nine ravens
that had convened above our heads . . .
a 'congress' or 'unkindness' named
by some, but let's call them a conjuring
due to the riddle read aloud the evening prior:
"what's the difference between a raven
and a writing desk?" We didn't know
that there is no difference . . . until
I gave you ravens by writing at this desk.

My Visitation

I stopped writing to become the poem.
               I stopped writing to become the poem.
A mourning dove phrases my losses.
               A mourning dove phrases my losses.

My losses stopped to become a mourning
dove writing the phrases I poem.

All that happened fades into forest.
               All that happened fades into forest,
a beginning for the page of another daybreak.
               A beginning for the page of another daybreak.

A page that happened fades into daybreak,
all for another beginning of the forest.

While the ground speaks of my visitation.
               While the ground speaks of my visitation,
story spores spread in mossy fruition.
               Story spores spread in mossy fruition.

Mossy spores of my visitation spread
ground while the story speaks in fruition.

To all that happened, daybreak.

        The page stopped. Story fades into spores,
        another beginning. A forest for my losses.

Phrases of a mourning dove spread in fruition.

        The ground speaks of the poem writing
        my visitation while mossy I become.

Afterward

Afternoon of flora, of fauna,
at a homestead greening. Spring—
where anything can crop up
after the melting, the last melting.

As April melds into May—
the cruelest month meets the merry.
A row of tulips unrolls, red after red,
beside an old shed with a low-slung roof.

Loudonville Reservoir on the other side
of a chain-link fence is out of bounds.
Hounds set to sic us if we cross over—
Cerberus numerous at the ready.

The shed is an easy climb for a coltish
girl. Settling on the rooftop, spread out
like the sky. Unleashing nebulous
stuff, daydreams—

like the one I had today at The Old
Lucketts Store. Liberating a life-sized
topiary horse—in transit from a ramshackle
cart to its rightful place.

The green horse, studded with rosettes
of *sempervivum* succulents, lands
next to the row of red tulips—like
a relic of an ice age that finally has thawed.

Notes

P. 18 "Future Plans" closes with a line from the song "Where Have All the Flowers Gone?" as recorded by Peter, Paul and Mary. Original lyrics are by Pete Seeger and Joe Hickerson.

P. 22 "Scene at the Tate" quotation source is John Everett Millais' letter to Mrs. Combe, July 2nd, 1851.

P. 26 "Flower Child" references my grandmother's shop, Burke's Florist, and Elvis Presley, a customer who ordered floral arrangements for his mother's grave.

P. 42 "Higher Ground" is inspired by the death of the poet Khet Thi, killed by the military junta of Myanmar. "Northbound Wild Elephant Eating and Walking Tour" was reported in *The Washington Post* (June 2, 2021).

P. 46 "Well-Read Rubáiyát" includes excerpts from *The Rubáiyát of Omar Khayyam* translated by Edward Fitzgerald.

P. 67 "Return" borrows its opening line from Walt Whitman's "Song of Myself, 52."

P. 74 "Canto do Poeta" is also the name of a Fado House in Lisbon.

P. 79 "Le Petit Prince" is an abecedarius inspired by the book *Le Petit Prince (The Little Prince)* by Antoine de Saint-Exupéry.

About the Author

Writer, performing artist, and board-certified dance / movement therapist Charise M. Hoge received her MA in Dance Therapy from New York University and her MSW from the University of Georgia. She is the author of *Striking Light from Ashes* (Finishing Line Press, 2017) and *Muse in a Suitcase* (Kelsay Books, 2021).

Her poetry is also featured in *Next Line, Please: Prompts to Inspire Poets and Writers* (edited by David Lehman, Cornell University Press, 2018), as well as notable literary journals. She is co-author of *Meet Your Muse: The Dance of Creativity* (Springtime Books, 2024) and *A Portable Identity: Your Guide to Taking Charge of Change Abroad* (Transition Press International, 2005, revised edition forthcoming).

Charise resides in the Washington, DC area and, at times, in the Appalachian Mountains—where she is poet-in-residence for the annual Art on Cullers Run (Mathias, West Virginia).

To find out more about her and her work, visit:
charisehoge.com

www.ingramcontent.com/pod-product-compliance
Lightning Source LLC
Chambersburg PA
CBHW030909170426
43193CB00009BA/794